HAL•LEONARD

JAZZ PLAY-ALONG

ok and CD for B♭, E♭, C and Bass Clef Instruments

volume
151

THE MODERN JAZZ QUARTET CLASSICS

Arranged and Produced by
Mark Taylor and Jim Roberts

BOOK

CD

ISBN 978-1-4234-9708-0

HAL•LEONARD
CORPORATION
7777 W. BLUEMOUND RD. P.O. BOX 13819 MILWAUKEE, WI 53213

Visit Hal Leonard Online at
www.halleonard.com

MODERN JAZZ QUARTET CLASSICS

Volume 151

Arranged and Produced by
Mark Taylor and Jim Roberts

Featured Players:

Graham Breedlove–Trumpet
John Desalme–Sax
Tony Nalker–Piano
Jim Roberts–Bass
Todd Harrison–Drums

Recorded at Bias Studios, Springfield, Virginia
Bob Dawson, Engineer

HOW TO USE THE CD:

Each song has <u>two</u> tracks:

1) Split Track/Melody

Woodwind, Brass, Keyboard, and **Mallet Players** can use this track as a learning tool for melody style and inflection.

Bass Players can learn and perform with this track – remove the recorded bass track by turning down the volume on the LEFT channel.

Keyboard and **Guitar Players** can learn and perform with this track – remove the recorded piano part by turning down the volume on the RIGHT channel.

2) Full Stereo Track

Soloists or **Groups** can learn and perform with this accompaniment track with the RHYTHM SECTION only.

4

BAG'S NEW GROOVE

BY MILT JACKSON

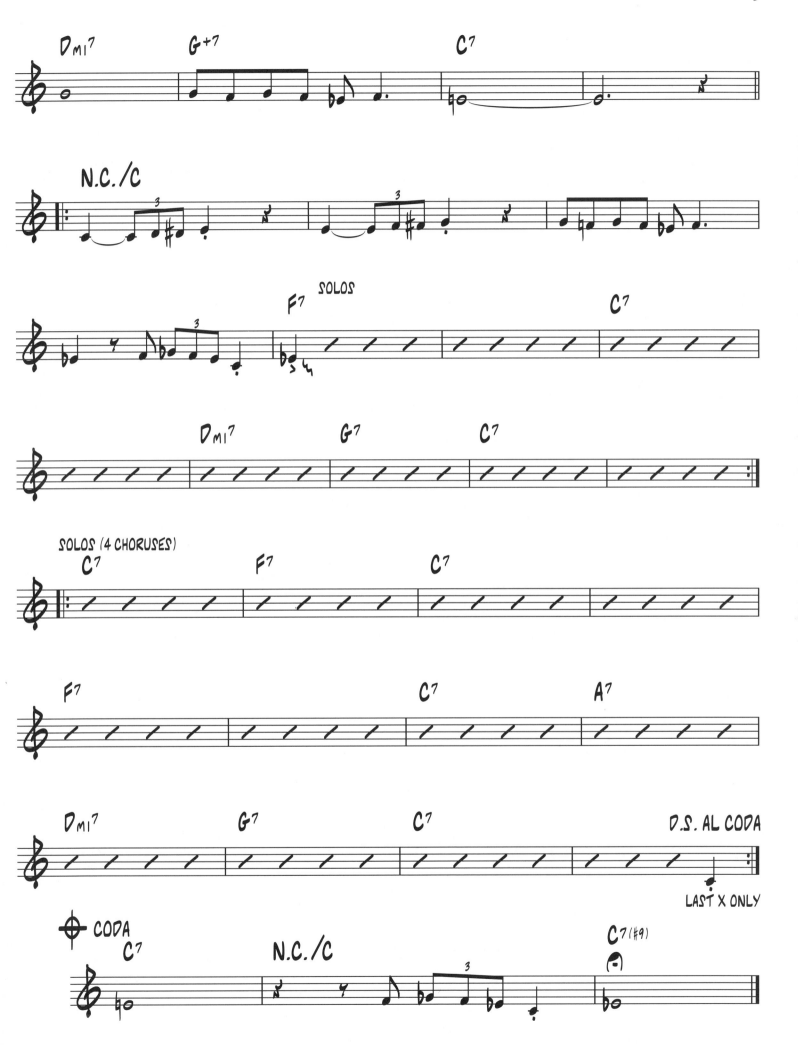

BAGS AND TRANE

BY MILT JACKSON

CD
◆3: SPLIT TRACK/MELODY
◆4: FULL STEREO TRACK

C VERSION

Blues in H (B)

BY MILT JACKSON

C VERSION

BLUES IN A MINOR

CD
◆ 5 : SPLIT TRACK/MELODY
◆ 6 : FULL STEREO TRACK

BY JOHN LEWIS

C VERSION
MEDIUM SWING

BLUESOLOGY

BY MILT JACKSON

DJANGO

BY JOHN LEWIS

C VERSION

CD

| 11 | : SPLIT TRACK/MELODY |
| 12 | : FULL STEREO TRACK |

DELAUNEY'S DILEMMA

BY JOHN LEWIS

C VERSION

13

THE GOLDEN STRIKER

BY JOHN LEWIS

C VERSION

CD
17 : SPLIT TRACK/MELODY
18 : FULL STEREO TRACK

La Ronde

BY JOHN LEWIS

C VERSION

VALERIA

BY JOHN LEWIS

VALERIA

BY JOHN LEWIS

: SPLIT TRACK/MELODY
: FULL STEREO TRACK

Bb VERSION

MEDIUM LATIN

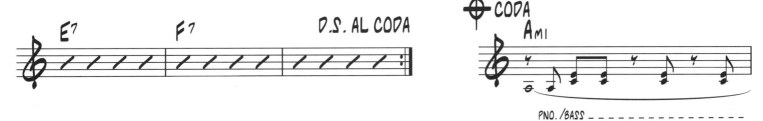

CD
1 : SPLIT TRACK/MELODY
2 : FULL STEREO TRACK

BAG'S NEW GROOVE

BY MILT JACKSON

Bb VERSION

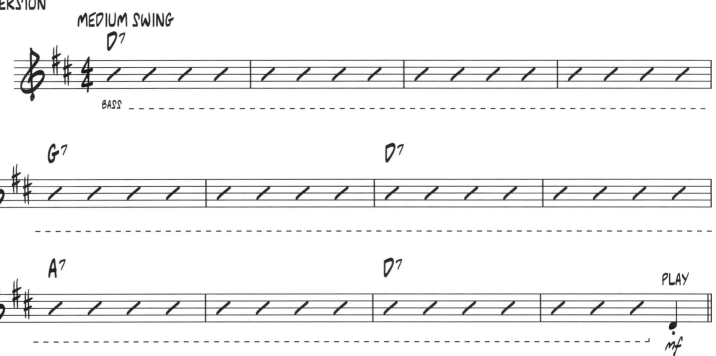

CD

BAGS AND TRANE

BY MILT JACKSON

Bb VERSION

Blues in H (B)

BY MILT JACKSON

Bb VERSION

BLUES IN A MINOR

BY JOHN LEWIS

Bb VERSION

BLUESOLOGY

BY MILT JACKSON

CD

9 : SPLIT TRACK/MELODY
10 : FULL STEREO TRACK

Bb VERSION

MEDIUM SWING

CD

◆13 : SPLIT TRACK/MELODY
◆14 : FULL STEREO TRACK

DJANGO

BY JOHN LEWIS

Bb VERSION

CD

🎵11: SPLIT TRACK/MELODY
🎵12: FULL STEREO TRACK

DELAUNEY'S DILEMMA

BY JOHN LEWIS

Bb VERSION

THE GOLDEN STRIKER

BY JOHN LEWIS

CD
15 : SPLIT TRACK/MELODY
16 : FULL STEREO TRACK

Bb VERSION

La Ronde

BY JOHN LEWIS

Bb VERSION

BAG'S NEW GROOVE

BY MILT JACKSON

CD

1 : SPLIT TRACK/MELODY
2 : FULL STEREO TRACK

Eb VERSION

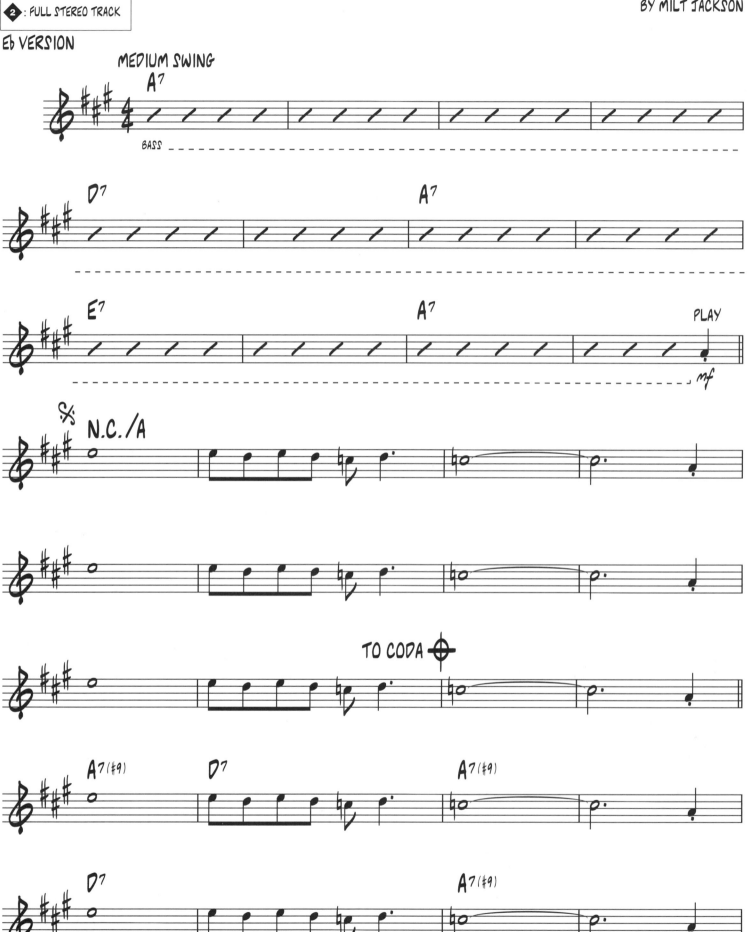

BAGS AND TRANE

BY MILT JACKSON

Eb VERSION

Blues in H (B)

BY MILT JACKSON

BLUES IN A MINOR

BY JOHN LEWIS

Eb VERSION

MEDIUM SWING
N.C.

PIANO

BASS SOLO

PLAY

F#mi   /E   D#mi7(b5) D6   F#mi/C# Bmi   F#mi7 G#mi7 A6 F#7/A#

Bmi   D7/C   C#7   F#mi7   G#mi7   A6   F#7/A#

Bmi7   D7/C   C#7   F#mi7

SOLOS (3 CHORUSES)
F#mi   F#mi7/E   D#mi7(b5) D6   F#mi/C# Bmi   F#mi7 G#mi7 A6 F#7/A#

Bmi   D7/C   C#7   F#mi7   G#mi7   A6   F#7/A#   Bmi7   D7/C

CD

9 : SPLIT TRACK/MELODY

10 : FULL STEREO TRACK

BLUESOLOGY

BY MILT JACKSON

Eb VERSION

Django

BY JOHN LEWIS

DELAUNEY'S DILEMMA

BY JOHN LEWIS

43

CD

THE GOLDEN STRIKER

BY JOHN LEWIS

Eb VERSION

CD

17 : SPLIT TRACK/MELODY
18 : FULL STEREO TRACK

LA RONDE

BY JOHN LEWIS

Eb VERSION

47

CD
19 : SPLIT TRACK/MELODY
20 : FULL STEREO TRACK

VALERIA

BY JOHN LEWIS

Eb VERSION

VALERIA

BY JOHN LEWIS

𝄢: C VERSION

MEDIUM LATIN

CD

1 : SPLIT TRACK/MELODY

2 : FULL STEREO TRACK

BAG'S NEW GROOVE

BY MILT JACKSON

51

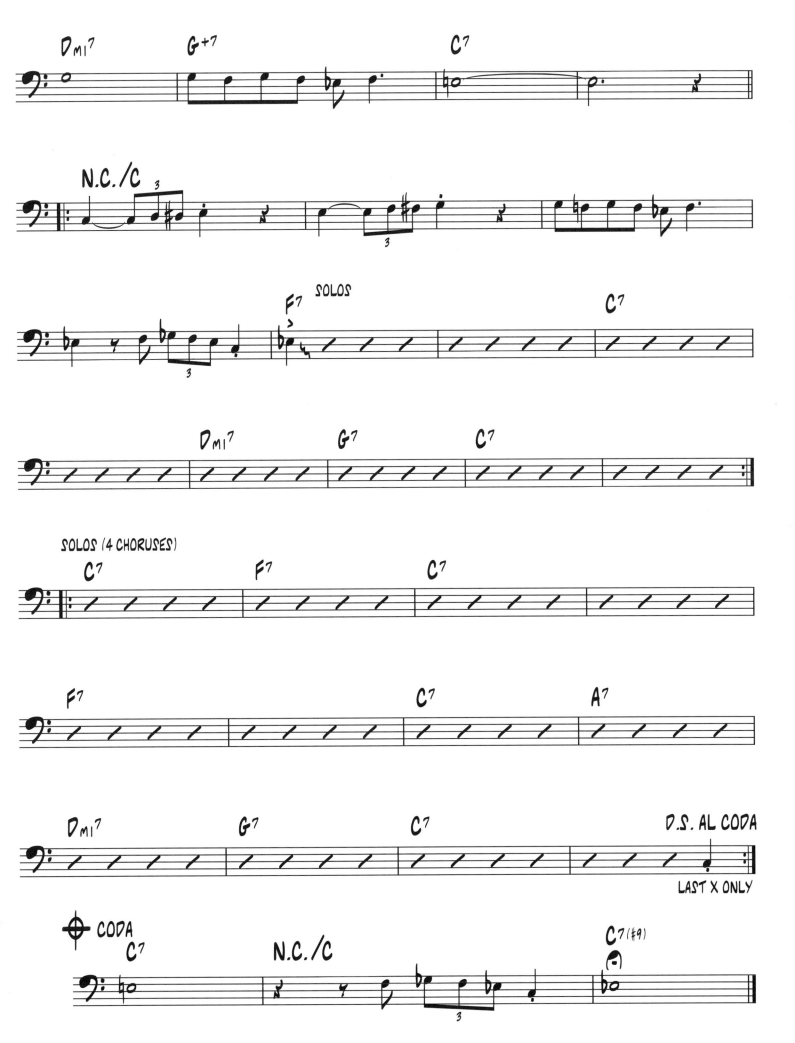

CD

- ◆ 3 : SPLIT TRACK/MELODY
- ◆ 4 : FULL STEREO TRACK

BAGS AND TRANE

BY MILT JACKSON

𝄢: C VERSION

Blues in H (B)

BY MILT JACKSON

♪: C VERSION

Blues in A Minor

: SPLIT TRACK/MELODY
: FULL STEREO TRACK

BY JOHN LEWIS

: C VERSION
MEDIUM SWING

Bluesology

BY MILT JACKSON

: SPLIT TRACK/MELODY
: FULL STEREO TRACK

🎵: C VERSION

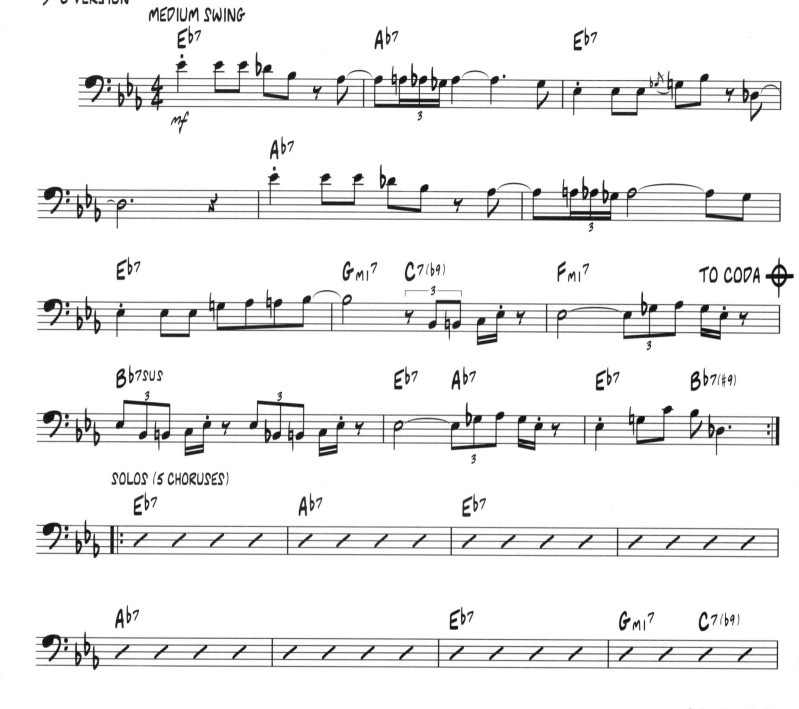

DJANGO

BY JOHN LEWIS

𝄢: C VERSION

DELAUNEY'S DILEMMA

BY JOHN LEWIS

59

THE GOLDEN STRIKER

BY JOHN LEWIS

CD
- 15 : SPLIT TRACK/MELODY
- 16 : FULL STEREO TRACK

𝄢: C VERSION

61

CD

17 : SPLIT TRACK/MELODY
18 : FULL STEREO TRACK

LA RONDE

BY JOHN LEWIS

𝄢: C VERSION

Presenting the Hal Leonard JAZZ PLAY-ALONG SERIES

Prices, contents, and availability
subject to change without notice.

FOR MORE INFORMATION,
SEE YOUR LOCAL MUSIC DEALER,
OR WRITE TO:

HAL•LEONARD®
CORPORATION

7777 W. BLUEMOUND RD. P.O. BOX 13819
MILWAUKEE, WISCONSIN 53213

Visit Hal Leonard online at
www.halleonard.com
for complete songlists.

0910